*To Say the Least*

# TO SAY THE LEAST

*Canadian Poets from A to Z*

*Edited by P.K. Page*

Press Porcépic Ltd.    Toronto

This edition is published by Press Porcépic Limited, with the assistance of the
Canada Council and the Ontario Arts Council.


Printed in Canada


**Canadian Cataloguing in Publication Data**

Main entry under titles:

To say the least

    ISBN 0-88878-174-1

    1. Canadian poetry.   I.   Page, Patricia K.,
1916-
PS8279.T6    C811′.008    C79-091156-6
PR9195.25.T6

Jerry Lampert, writer and friend of writers, died too young in 1978.

Those of us who knew him have wanted to establish and contribute to a Gerald Lampert Memorial Fund to be administered by his widow, Arlene. At her wish the fund will finance an annual scholarship for a young writer.

Selections from the work of 102 poets appear in this book. All those contacted, and in some cases their estates or publishers, have generously waived their permission fees and all royalties have been assigned to the fund.

For Arthur
a man of few words
with love

## Introduction

This book began as three short poems: *For Anne*, by Leonard Cohen, *"I am almost asleep,"* by Eldon Grier and *Is*, by F.R. Scott. It was entirely memorable. I carried it around in my head.

Little by little the collection grew—the three poems became six: Dorothy Livesay's *Going to Sleep*, Elizabeth Gourlay's *Skeleton Wish*, John Newlove's *Complaint*. Before long I had a head full of them—none longer than twelve lines—passionate, profound, powerful, wicked, witty, wise. An anthology.

If, at the beginning, I had certain pre-conceived notions about short poems—that they lend themselves most readily to epigrams and conceits and to haiku-like descriptions, for instance, but not to narrative verse or to conveying time's duration—I have no such notions now. There are poems here which demolish these ideas, poems which establish that the short poem can be larger than its mass. Which is one of the reasons why it is so often memorable.

In putting the book together I tried as a sculptor does to sense the form hidden in his material and, in bringing it to light, give significant shape to the whole. Within that shape I have tried too, to create an order in which each poem is linked to its immediate neighbours in such a way as to augment them. This linkage, sometimes logical, sometimes not, is never random. For me at least, the whole is greater than the sum of its parts and this suggests that the book should be read from first to last, as it was designed.

All the poems are by Canadians or have been published in Canada. Astonishingly, their authors constitute an entire alphabet of poets—from A to Z. I hope that for even the most avid poetry reader they will offer some surprises.

P.K. Page

star fish
fish star

*Phyllis Webb*

## Of Skies

Goldfish, stars of the pond.
I loiter above their sky
Our worlds upturned.

*Mike Doyle*


## Play Among The Stars

Every noon
I cook two eggs

seeking the variations
that speak of

a higher galaxy
in any menial action

done right, done
with grace, done

as lovely as these two
sunny side up.

*George Bowering*

## Spaces

The seven stars
of the Great Wain
hang in the sky
a million light years
one from another
and from me, but I
gather the seven together
who could never know
me or one another
but for my human eye.

*Louis Dudek*

## Falling Star

As a boy, having been sent
to bed in the afternoon:

rebelliously pushing on
the bedroom window till it

fell like a crashing star
flying from my hands,

suddenly to be arranged
over the earth like a jig

saw puzzle & leaving
behind a rent in the sky

*C.H. Gervais*

## ❧ The Tree

The TREE

A record when a tree's cut down?
A stone thrown into a pond?
No,      planets orbiting our sun.

Yes, night-sky's a forest.
Each tree has a star core.

Once before I woke I reached
A path where you can touch
Our rough furrowed skin & bark

Inside which rind we sleeping are,

James Reaney

## Suns and Planets

Suns and planets of the sky
When will you be ripe and die?
Will a great wind sometime sweep
The dark branches where you weep
And dash and pluck and throw
Venus and Mars and grey Pluto
Like pears, apples and plums upon the ground
(Red, yellow and gold, oval and round)
To grow mildewed and ragged there
Softening the thick autumn air
With your piebald rays' decay?

*James Reaney*


## Keys

Wanting to write a poem, I
walk around all day with the
tips of my fingers wide open

touch touch touch

a star at each tip

run home, let them press
into the keyboard

*David McFadden*

## From *Three Poems about Poets*

Poets are fishermen crying
'Fresh catch from sleep,
Fresh as the mackerel sky
Or a salmon's leap
Is the catch we offer.
Come buy, come buy!'

*Anne Wilkinson*


## *This is Not*

this is not
        my poetry
i do not conceive
        then
        write it.
it is the work
        of a
small inexhaustible demon
who grinds my bones
        into verse.

*Deborah Gore*

## Mice in the House

One of them scampers down the curtain
and up to my motionless feet—
I have the feeling watching that
representatives of two powerful races
are meeting here calmly as equals—
But the mouse will not be damn fool enough
                    to go away and write a poem.

*Al Purdy*


## 'I am almost asleep'

I am almost asleep
with your poems on my chest,

Apollinaire

I am almost asleep,
but I feel a transfusion of fine little letters
dripping slantwise into my side.

*Eldon Grier*

### 🏃 Poetry for Intellectuals

If you say in a poem "grass is green",
They all ask, "What did you mean?"

"That nature is ignorant," you reply,
"And on a deeper level—youth must die."

If you say in a poem "grass is red",
They understand what you have said.

*Louis Dudek*

### 🏃 Poetry

In this intangible art, the wish
is not father
to the deed, which is
the beauty of it.

*Jerry Newman*

## Poets & Muses

Poets are such bad employers,
Muses ought to Organize:
Time off, sick pay, danger wages—
Come, ye wretched of the skies!

Poets, to reverse the story,
Muse-redeemed, return and live:
Solomon in all his glory
Could not pay for what you give.

*Jay Macpherson*


## The Muses' Cradle

From childhood's cradle I have shaped this other,
Where sleeps my Muse while birdsong trills above her,
My white-robed Muse, my one and only dear!

Those golden kisses at day's kindly close...
But hush! already at our door I hear
The harridan Distress creak her black shoes.

*Emile Nelligan*
*Trans. P.F. Widdows*

## Biography

Out of the sea I took you, laid my mouth
against your mouth and fed you with my breath
Sea lark, imaginary girl
who now insists on being real

*Alden Nowlan*


## More Intricate

More intricate
than ferns,
the keys of being.

Before this writing
you stood opaque.

My poem and
now this
suddenness of seeing.

*Milton Acorn*

### From *Three Poems about Poets*

Poets are cool as the divers who wander
The floor of the sea;
Their eyes are aquariums, swimming
With starfish and stranger.

Dark waters breed the phantoms
They haul in their nets to the sun
And sun is the power
That glisters their scales with meaning.

  *Anne Wilkinson*



The sunshine is the glee
of all us little things.

  *Christian Schenk*
  *aged 9*

## Sunstroke. 1954

In the blaze
of noon
I was wax
and melted
with the authority
of an Icarus.

But later
my skin radiated
mythic wings
which
through the night
connected me
with sun.

*Gail Fox*

## Sitting

The degree of nothingness
is important:
to sit emptily
in the sun
receiving fire
that is the way
to mend
an extraordinary world,
sitting perfectly
still
and only
remotely human.

*Phyllis Webb*

## Fog

The morning is foggy.
Cars drive silently to work.
A woman walks through snow
a coat without a face.

It will be difficult this morning
to manage to see the sun rise.

*Elizabeth Brewster*

## Ni *la Mort ni le Soleil*
(On a maxim of de la Rochefoucauld)

Neither on death, nor at the blazing sun
Can mortal gaze
Without being blinded by the one
As by the other's rays:
They are two fascinations eyes reject,
Looking, yet loth
To fix themselves upon the sight elect—
Brightworlds both.

*A. M. Klein*

## *Eclipse*

I looked the sun straight in the eye.
He put on dark glasses.

*F. R. Scott*

### 𐘳  Moon Phases

an orange

one bite
CHOMP! CHOMP!

another

all gone

black orange

    *Mike Doyle*


### 𐘳  moon: tracks

i can't say where the rails lead
the moon's white light

except that they go to dark horizons
and over.

    *D. M. Price*

## From *Binaries*

Soul, clap your hands,
　　But do not sing;
Your angel flies
　　On raven wing.

*George Woodcock*


## The Plowman in Darkness

You ask for the Plowman:
He's as much
In the dark as you are—
Moves by touch,
Stubbing his toes
From age to age
Is working up a
Snorting rage,
Swears he'll beat his plowshare
Into a sword
Come the great and harrowing
Day of the Lord.

*Jay Macpherson*

## La Belle Dame sans dormi

She did not dream
Except to wear
A word across her groin
She wore no jewels
But the snake
Living on her arm
She could not sleep
For sleep would watch
The flies stroll on her face
She did not dare
To lose her web
In that dark webbed place.

*Anne Wilkinson*


## Grace For Snow

I prayed to you for sleep, for silence
from the night-voices and peace
from the night-faces.
You sent cloth in thick folds to cover and close
the shiny black eye of the night's window.
I prayed to you for a blessing, for grace
from the slow scream of the city's sorrow.
You sent snow.

*Jeni Couzyn*

## A Dream

A street at night,
winter's first snow,
I sense movements
about us, dim horses
circling.
My mind cannot hold
those pale horses,
my head
heavy in a dark helmet.

*Ian Young*

## From *Translations from the Japanese*

The fireflies,
pursued,
hide themselves
in the moonlight.

*W. W. E. Ross*

## 🐾 From *Non Linear*

My white skin
is not the moonlight.
If it is
tell me, who reads
by that light?

*Phyllis Webb*

## 🐾 *Like a Garment*

On the pale sand
my sea-drenched body
like a garment lies

I am far gone with light

*Kay Smith*

## 🐦 Fabulous Shadow

They fished me from this Quebec river
the face blurred glass, bones of wing
draping my body like nets
in a patterned butterfly

and peeled green weed from scorched shoulders
and the dried wax from my thighs

*Michael Ondaatje*



## 🐦 Divine Image

Swiftly darting in the setting light
The doomed sparrow feels the falcon's wings.
How beautiful are they both in flight.

*Irving Layton*

*Blues*

*bpNichol*

you fit into me
like a hook into an eye

a fish hook
an open eye

*Margaret Atwood*

## *Oppression*

Oppression is
convincing someone
that only
you can
truly serve
them and
that you
are wanting
nothing in
return nothing
in return

*Robert Sward*

## *Seymour Inlet Float Camp:*
## *Domestic Scene*

mother is sewing
father's
thumb back on

*John Marshall*

## 𓅓 Stabilities

She: bedridden
He: bedrock

*Penny Kemp*


## 𓅓 *View of a Madhouse*

Curving downward in front of the window
where they have lain my lady
an awning is slowly lowered
away out toward me and over—

hair thrown forward—
above her head
baring her nape

as the whole scene falls on its knees

*R. G. Everson*

## Mad Boy's Song

The small activity of mice,
The velvet passing of a moth,
And one grey spider's cautious tread
Make thunder in this shed:
Where God has stored his tightened drum—
A mind inside a head!

*Leo Kennedy*

## They Say I do not Suffer

They say I do not suffer
But who thinks my thoughts
Who labors my day for me
Who loses strength
Who falls
Who kneels
For whom is night a torture
Who bleeds in my dreams?

*Waclaw Iwaniuk*
*Trans. Jagna Boraks*

*Trinity*

Imprisoned in a Liverpool of self
I haunt the gutted arcades of the past.
Where it lies on some high forgotten shelf
I find what I was looking for at last.
But now the shelf has turned into a mast
And now the mast into an upturned tree
Where one sways crucified twixt two of me.

*Malcolm Lowry*

From little sorrows little poems come;
When grief is great the stricken heart is dumb.

*A.J.M. Smith*

## The Search

In Dante no, in Shakespeare no.
Nor yet in any library you go.
And in His book you scarcely dare
To hope you'll find your agony there.

*Malcolm Lowry*


## Strange Type

I wrote: in the dark cavern of our birth.
The printer had it tavern, which seems better.
But herein lies the subject of our mirth,
Since on the next page death appears as dearth.
So it may be that God's word was distraction,
Which to our strange type appears destruction,
Which is bitter.

*Malcolm Lowry*

## Aunt Jane

Aunt Jane of whom I dreamed the nights it thundered,
was dead at ninety, buried at a hundred.
We kept her corpse a decade, hid upstairs,
where it ate porridge, slept and said its prayers.

And every night before I went to bed
they took me in to worship with the dead.
Christ Lord, if I should die before I wake,
I pray thee Lord my body take.

*Alden Nowlan*

## Hanging

High on the tree one apple alone
All her golden companions withered and gone.

*Elizabeth Gourlay*

## The Sibyl at Cumae

I saw the Sibyl at Cumae,
where she was hung up
in a bottle.

The children would ask her,
"What do you want, Sibyl?"

And she would always answer,
"I want to die."

John Robert Colombo
Found in the Screenplay to
Fellini's *Satyricon* (1969)


## Aria Senza da Capo

The stork questioned the swan whose moving song
Was more than usually sweet and long:
What's the good news? You'd think you were a lark!
I'm going to die, the swan answered the stork.

*Robert Finch*

## A Dying Man

Some compulsion to ask:
"Is there anything you want?"

afraid of his answer
for there's nothing I can give,

ashamed of my question
knowing he knows,

forgiven by a lie,
his merciful, "No."

*Gael Turnbull*

## If you should die

If you should die
I'd give my flesh
For purposes of worms
And ivory grow my bones
And moss my hair

Until I grew desirable
To death
And you moved over
And we shared the earth

*Anne Wilkinson*

## ❧  The Sickness unto Death

Death's emissary came
And said, Why Not?
I hesitated a fateful second
And was caught.

*Jerry Newman*

## ❧  Ongoing

A green such a green o quivers
in a green sign across the street. I sit
at the customer's side of a desk, bargaining
for the least funeral. The undertaker
wavers, leaning toward my case.
We are in company with death, we two,
but the ongoing has its hook in us.

*George Johnston*

## 🎋 *Epitaph*

Malcolm Lowry
Late of the Bowery
His prose was flowery
And often glowery
He lived nightly, and drank daily,
And died playing the ukelele.

*Malcolm Lowry*

## 🎋 *A Farmer's Epitaph*

Deep night upholds the heavy doom
Of roses over Shepherd's tomb,
And he who tore the acre lies
Where brain knows no Spring ecstasies.
In six by two of blue-green clay
Earth has her still revenge today.

*George Woodcock*

## Beside One Dead

This is the sheath,
   the sword drawn,
These are the lips,
   the word spoken.
This is Calvary
   toward dawn;
And this is the
   third-day token—
The opened tomb
   and the Lord gone:
Something whole
   that was broken.

*A.J.M. Smith*


## Requiescat

The tiny wristwatch stopped ticking
and died
and grew as cold as cuff-links
and tie-pins and bracelets
and necklaces and earrings and brooches
and diadems. . . .

*Robert Zend*

## Razor Blade

i looked at the razor blade.
the razor blade looked at me.
i liked its coldness.
it liked my warm wrist.
in a red ceremony,
i married the razor blade;
the razor blade married me.

*Deborah Gore*

## Going to Sleep

I shall lie like this when I am dead—
But with one more secret in my head.

*Dorothy Livesay*

After all

Crazy Jane might have said
we all
struggle upward
into grace

and

after all
she might have said
we all
lie down
at last
in the same
broad bed

*Rona Murray*

##  *Unfinished Poem*

Bring me black slippers.
The corpse would dance.

*Alden Nowlan*

I too am a student
I'm learning dying

*Robin Skelton*

 *First and Last*

I was born on August 4th 1945,
and on August 5th,
while I suckled in tranquility,
Hiroshima played host
to the first Atomic Bomb.
God, to think of all those people
who woke with me,
only once.

*Joseph Sherman*

## The Cloud

Why does my mind keep returning
to the long morning
staring at the wall
the cloudless morning when nobody worked
when nobody talked or nobody heard them
a day without pity or anger
alone with the one thought
we      did      that

Why do my thoughts keep to the one track?
What are they trying to hide?
Why do they always go back
to Hiroshima?

*Francis Sparshott*


## Alchemist

Man, the evil magician,
brews, in the perishable cauldron
of rock and sand,
a violent, fiery potion,
melted lightning.

Foolish enchanter,
do not break
this great brown dish
with green edges
which has been in the family
all these years.
Where will you find another
to hold your children's supper?

*Elizabeth Brewster*

## 𝕫ᵖ Anxious

Anxious
of course I'm anxious
afraid
of course I'm afraid
I don't know what about
I don't know what of
but I'm afraid
and I feel it's
right to be.

*Miriam Waddington*


## 𝕫ᵖ Greener than Nature

It's a time of prevailing breasts
in the fields of pleasure

the plundering hand takes its honey
from the heart of the original hive

the clover is bitter
and the sun has a face of wax

*Roland Giguère*
*Trans. F.R. Scott*

## Voices

I am aware of a locked world within myself
I can feel things struggling to be free

Sometimes a strangled word enters my mouth
Wax plugs my ears my mind refuses to move

I sit silently hoping the sound will die down
I am frightened I shall try to get through to me

After all I still have some rights here
This is a miracle I know nothing about

*Doug Beardsley*


## Corridor Smiles

He gives me
a smile

telling me
he hates
himself

I smile back
but do not love
myself

enough yet
to love him

*Mike Doyle*

How many times
      a meeting has struck barriers
            cement blocks
               in me

heart of stone
heart of stone
      unable to listen
         i fear
         and fly by
who can liberate me from myself?

*Jean Vanier*

## 🌿 *Morning*

Sometime
Somewhere
Someone
was
but when I woke I forgot who

*Robert Zend*

## We are not One

—We are not one but two
we are not two but four
we are not four but many
and sometimes
we are not any—

Miriam Waddington

## From The Great Bear Lake Meditations

The wolves say to the dogs
what the madman of me says to
the citizen.
I need to go fishing until
I need to return.

J. Michael Yates

## On Brushing my Hair in the Static-Filled Air

How stubborn the parts of the body!
Will     or     Won't

Hair what it wishes
Mind where it wills
incendiary Heart

Who is this impotent I
this King Canute?

*P.K. Page*


## Witness to my Body

I am witness to my body,
A gift, unsolicited, that seems
At times nothing of me,
Strips of being, put together

Without thought, without art.
And my speech is a dialect
Of strange tongues which are
Incomprehensible to each other.

*R.A.D. Ford*

## From *Poems in Braille*

with legs and arms I make alphabets
like in those children's books
where people bend into letters and signs,
yet I do not read the long cabbala of my bones
truthfully; I need only to move
to alter the design

*Gwendolyn MacEwen*

## O Earth, Turn!

The little blessed Earth that turns
Does so on its own concerns
As though it weren't my home at all;
It turns me winter, summer, fall
Without a thought of me.

I love the slightly flattened sphere,
Its restless, wrinkled crust's my here,
Its slightly wobbling spin's my now
But not my why and not my how:
My why and how are me.

*George Johnston*

## 🌱 The Cabbage

The doctor goes on handing out pills
that reduce me
from animal
to vegetable

Why couldn't he
implant some sunflower seeds
so at least I'd be able to see
over the fence?

*Dorothy Livesay*


## 🌱 Illusion from my Speedy Car

A white-blossoming nightgown pear-tree
runs through glooms of leafless oak,
escaping in virtue the dingy wilderness.

*R. G. Everson*

## Field in the Wind

The grass is running in the wind
Without a sound,
Crouching and smooth and fast
Along the ground.
The clouds run too,
And little shadows play
And scurry in the grass
That will not stay
But runs and runs, until
The wind is still.

*Floris Clark McLaren*


## Ellesmereland

Explorers say that harebells rise
from the cracks of Ellesmereland
and cod swim fat beneath the ice
that grinds its meagre sands
No man is settled on that coast
The harebells are alone
Nor is there talk of making man
from ice cod bell or stone

*Earle Birney*

## 🌿 The Wind Disturbs

—the wind disturbs
below the waterfall
      the harebells
           and
wild columbine.

*D. G. Jones*


## 🌿 At the Bottom of the Dark

At the bottom of the dark
I woke to hear the rustling of the curtains
           of the rain and a bird singing

*Kay Smith*

No temple or palace, no apartment house,
Neither Chartres nor the glass combs of Chicago
Glittering on Michigan Drive, can compare
With the intricate architecture
In which the birds reside.

D. G. Jones

## Song

The sun is mine
And the trees are mine
The light breeze is mine
And the birds that inhabit the air
are mine
Their voices upon the wind
are in my ear

Robert Hogg

## THE HAT

Against me wears the wind a coat
And to protect her from your feet
Ma Earth puts on a dusty shoe
Rain against him taps a roof
Against me puts the Sun a hat

Hey you! Tramp! When is it that
You'll take off your dusty shoes
& hang up your coat & hat

Child, listen: that will be
When in my tramping, weeping, searching

I have found    A river to the sea.

*James Reaney*

## Song

What a wonderful way
To come into the city
All over the bridge

O

   ver

      the bridge.

*Fred Wah*


## Tree in a Street

Why will not that tree adapt itself to our tempo?
We have lopped off several branches,
cut her skin to the white bone,
run wires through her body and her loins,
yet she will not change.
Ignorant of traffic, of dynamos and steel,
as uncontemporary
as bloomers and bustles
she stands there like a green cliché.

*Louis Dudek*

## 🌿 XXX

Is a tree kinder
Than a doormat?
Kinder than the little worn corners
Trodden all to pieces?

I have seen housemaids beating doormats.
Housemaids do not beat trees.
Neither do dogs sleep in trees.
But I have seen dogs sleeping on doormats.

Trees have only birds, and insects, and crawly things.
There is no vulgarity in these,
Only poetry, and evolution, and innumerable legs.
But in doormats. . .

X

### 🌿 Streetlights

they're not sunflowers
yet they burn on their stems
like the golden eyes of those other plants

and they bend
in such an iron complaint
toward the street's inverted sky

I'd like to think
they know as much of final things
as any living creature who endures the dark.

*Eli Mandel*


### 🌿 Nocturne in Burrard Inlet

Church bells are chiming on the rail
And wheels the frightful killer whale
The gulls are baaing in the creek
And night is whetting up its beak. . .

*Malcolm Lowry*

## ⚘ *Pattern*

All rapids are redeemed:
The dark isolate oxbows,
Those exiled directions,
Lost rivers
Turning back the last light,
Like old animals staggered from the herd,
In wait for whatever is theirs alone.

*W.D. Ulrich*

## ⚘ *First Night of Fall, Grosvenor Ave.*

In the blue lamplight
the leaf falls

on its shadow

*George Bowering*

## Aesthetic Curiosity

Does an owl appreciate
The color of leaves
As they fall about him
In the staggering nights of Autumn?

*A.M. Klein*


## The Street in Fall

Apocalypse of leaves
emerald, gold, blood color;

the town all around me
and in my head;

I am stilled by the let-go
the stems give.

*George Johnston*

## 𝄢 Fall

A stiff breeze shakes the summer
Red-blistered leaves rake into piles
A spark sheds black ash everywhere

The first snow guards the hillside
Like the white wrist of winter
The fist is not far behind

*Doug Beardsley*

## 𝄢 The Frost

But the morning
hoar frost

the breath of cold birds
on trees

the metal of January
in this place.

The crystals, white
hanging from the iron handrail

cold to fingers
sweet to taste

*George Bowering*

### Munchausen in Alberta

Our first winter in the settlement,
the old man said,
January was so cold
the flames in the lamp froze.
The women picked them like strawberries
and gave them to the children to eat.

That's the only time
I was ever a fire-eater.

*Elizabeth Brewster*

## Lake Harvest

Down on the flat of the lake
Out on the slate and the green,
Spotting the border of Erie's sleeping robe of silver-blue
                        changeable silk,
In sight of the shimmer of silver-blue changeable silk,
In the sun
The men are sawing the frosted crystal,
Patient the horses look on from the sleighs,
Patient the trees, down from the bank, darkly ignoring
                        the sun.
Each saw sings and whines in a gray-mittened hand,
And diamonds and pieces of a hundred rainbows are strown
                        around.

*Raymond Knister*

## 🌿 *Snow*

Snow puts us in a dream on vast plains without track or colour

Beware, my heart, snow puts us in the saddle on steeds of foam

Proclaim the coronation of childhood, snow consecrates us on high seas, dreams fulfilled, all sails set

Snow puts us in a trance, a widespread whiteness, flaring plumes pierced by the red eye of this bird

My heart; a point of fire under palms of frost flows the marvelling blood.

*Anne Hébert*
*Trans. F.R. Scott*

🌿 *Canada in winter:*

Canada in wooden crates
that fish come in, frozen.

*Jill Hoffman*


🌿 *Frost*

frost on my window
night comes creaking up

close
stars crowd

*George Johnston*

## Deep

My walls bend over me
and my dolls and my creatures;
there is frost on the window,
we can hardly see out,

and quietly all night
 the snow,
don't feel it in my sleep
but down down one flake after another
 deep.

*George Johnston*

## White Mountain

Trees in glass robes
cold under the moon's cowl.
Arms hold ice.

Wind carries only the howl
of a dog. Ashes of snow
in grey fire.

There is only a faint glow.
Roads of men advance
and retreat.

Tracks fill with snow.

*Patrick Lane*

Tiretracks
        in snow
thread filet popcorn picot
lace on bobbin
wheeled roads
        unwinding
white swags complicate
crystalline simplicities
        as witness
in the pure fields:   footprints
drop catspaw doilies trim
as a spinster's parlor, stars
turned antimacassars.

*Phyllis Gotlieb*


## Winter Sparrows

Feathered leaves
    on a leafless bush.
Dropping to feed
    they fly back to the stems.

*F.R. Scott*

## February

I wonder about
the worms & the ants—

will they ever
come alive again?

*Nelson Ball*


## Catpath

Black on Mrs Crowder's post
    watching
tabby on Mr Moir's post
    watching
Mrs Osborn's bullhead marmalade tom
footing along the catpath in the snow.

*George Johnston*

## A Cat

A white cat
By a window
From its bench
Sniffs and watches
Watches for the wind
And watches for the rain
Watches like a white cat
For the black cat of pain

*Jacques Godbout*
*Trans. J.R. Colombo*

## On a Cat's Portrait

The Egyptian lapis cat
in the Louvre
shapes out divinity.
Goya's cat scowls
demoniac.

My cat, black-and-white
in art as in nature,
thrusts the forepaw imperial
like the Shanghai British lion
whose mane is worn smooth
by the secretive palms
of luck-seeking proletarians.

*George Woodcock*

Cézanne at last was tempted by an apple
To forgo women and with fruit to grapple.

*Goodridge Roberts*


## Life Work

I am an artist, who, for forty years
Has stood at the lake edge
Throwing stones in the lake.
Sometimes, very faintly,
I hear a splash.

*Maxwell Bates*

## Let Us Rebuild
(Translated from the French of Max Jacob)

It is enough that a child of five, in pale blue blouse,
should draw pictures in an album for a door to open
into the light, for the castle to be rebuilt, and the dry
brown of the hillside to be covered with flowers.

*W.W.E. Ross*


## Epitaph
(For Arthur Lismer)

Where his foot
  went first
    you freely
      now may
        walk

It is this
  door he
    opened

It is your
  door

*F.R. Scott*

### From *Epitre à Monsieur Labadie*

Say, Artist, what's the hardest sentence known?
To be applauded by your Friends alone.

> *Joseph Quesnel*
> *Trans. John Glassco*

### From *Outmoded Wisdom*

#### *Cleobulus*

To bring mine enemy down in black despair,
I prayed, "May the gods grant his every prayer."

> *L. A. MacKay*

## Of Faith, Hope, and Charity

Beware,—spiritual humankind,—
Faith, contraceptive of the mind;
And hope, cheap aphrodisiac,
Supplying potency its lack;
And also that smug lechery
Barren and sterile charity.

*A. M. Klein*


## Epigram for A. M. Klein

They say you keep the devils laughing by your wit
And all the furnaces stilled that they may hear it

*Irving Layton*

## 🐦 An Aristocratic Trio

'Mongst illustrious men in the Bible there be
King Domcome, Lord Howlong, and Baron Fig-tree.

*Judson France*


## 🐦 Prussian Blue

What shall ignorant men say:
Was it Accident or Fate
Or some powerfuller thing
More sinister than they
Which ordained Frederick the Great
Choose for his regal bedmate
Queens whose names commence with K
—Keith, Katte, and Keyserlingk?

*Irving Layton*

## 🌿 Love

Girl: Hickory Dickory
Boy: Dock.

*Jeni Couzyn*

## 🌿 *Yes and No*

Yes opens to the sky its asking arms
And funnels to an I
Cascades of joy.

But crooked No keeps poking with his nose
A blinding zero.
                    Round and round he goes.

*F.R. Scott*

## Lines for a Bookmark

You who read. . .
May you seek
As you look;
May you keep
What you need;
May you care
What you choose;
And know here
In this book
Something strange,
Something sure,
That will change
You and be yours.

*Gael Turnbull*


## Egg

Reader, in your hand you hold
A silver case, a box of gold.
I have no door, however small,
Unless you pierce my tender wall,
And there's no skill in healing then
Shall ever make me whole again.
Show pity, Reader, for my plight:
Let be, or else consume me quite.

*Jay Macpherson*

O
is
this
a bell
enough bell
no
?

*Bell*

*Colleen Thibaudeau*


*I*
*AM A*
*TINY*
*SPINNING TOP*
*NOW IN A RHYME*
*HOW CAN I STOP*
*? ? ? ? ? ? ?*
*????????*
*? ? ?*
*?*

*The Top*

*Colleen Thibaudeau*

## 'Go Take the World'

Go take the world my dearest wish
And blessing, little book.
And should one ask who's in the dish
Or how the beast was took,
Say: Wisdom is a silver fish
And Love a golden hook.

*Jay Macpherson*


## To Jay Macpherson
## On Her Book of Poems

Dear no-man's-nightingale, our Fisher Queen,
Whose golden hook makes muddy waters green,
With what dexterity of wrist and eye
You flick the willow-rod and cast the fly;
And when the silver fish is caught and drawn,
How neat the table he's divided on,
How white the cloth, how elegant the dish,
How sweet the flesh—O sacramental Fish!

*A.J.M. Smith*

# Of Nothing at All: Orders

Muffle the wind;
Silence the clock;
Muzzle the mice;
Curb the small talk;
Cure the hinge-squeak;
Banish the thunder.
Let me sit silent,
Let me wonder.

*A. M. Klein*


# Is

Is
is not
the end of Was
or start
of Will Be
Is
is
Is.

*F. R. Scott*

## 🏃 *The Two Sides of a Drum*

When Night lets down her hair
Over the pale blossoms
Of the world, far, far from here,
With sealed eyes, still bosom
And folded feet I fare
To that country under dream
Where eternity and time
Are the two sides of a drum.

*A.J.M. Smith*

## 🏃 *For Margaret*

The years—the sunny and the dappled and the shadowed years
And Time, the only maker and the sure destroyer of us all.

*Howard O'Hagan*

## Story

Let us begin with Death
Overheard, in the cry
Of the first breath,

That for what it is worth,
We may all thereby
End with Birth.

*Richard Outram*

## The Well

A winter hanging over the dark well,
My back turned to the sky,
To see if in that blackness something stirs,
Or glints, or winks an eye:

Or, from the bottom looking up, I see
Sky's white, my pupil head—
Lying with all that's lost, with all that shines—
My winter with the dead:

A well of truth, of images, of words.
Low where Orion lies
I watch the solstice pit become a stair,
The constellations rise.

*Jay Macpherson*

## The Reborn

Shadows eat the leaves
and the wind rings with fear.
Emptiness holds me like a child.

Mother of darkness
I have poured my soul like water.
Change me!

The earth opens.
The head, sweet as a berry,
swivels in the sun-glow.

Dearest child of the warm lips,
you have given me myself.
I will become what I am.

*Rosemary Sullivan*


## Old Adam

My old man had a rib in his side.
It was his sorrow and his pride.
I took it from him while he snored.
In his dream old Adam roared,
And when he woke he wept to see,
Of pride and sorrow I'd made me.

*Anne Wilkinson*

## ❧ Farewell

I see you walking down beyond that knoll

> Your bare legs are gone
> now your young girl body
> your face
> waving arm
> hand

I have disappeared into the ground

> *R. G. Everson*


## ❧ Running Child

watching my running child
on her seventh summer's beach
I see that other child
incredulously allowed back
through the afternoon's haze
to run beside her
turning his head towards her
to gauge his joy

thirty years ago

> *Don Coles*

## Stefan

Stefan
aged eleven
looked at the baby and said
*When he thinks it must be pure thought*
*because he hasn't any words yet*
and we
proud parents
admiring friends
who had looked at the baby

looked at the baby again

*P.K. Page*

## Hannah

Her third eye is strawberry jam
has a little iris in it
her eyelids
         are red
she's sleepy
    and the milk
       has gone down
          the wrong way.
I've just had breakfast
with the smallest person in the world.

*Robert Sward*

## The Third Eye

Of three eyes I would still give two for one.
The third eye clouds: its light is nearly gone.
The two saw green, saw sky, saw people pass:
The third eye saw through order like a glass
To concentrate, refine and rarify
And make a Cosmos of miscellany.
Sight, world and all to save alive that one
Fading so fast! Ah love, its light is done.

*Jay Macpherson*


## A Drink in the Luxembourg

Reflected violets fall, a crystal barrow
Navigates the *agent's* traffic block
Where cupids underpin the soaring fountain
And calm furred children sail beneath the clock.

O see, the noon light strikes into the circle!
Shattered, it splinters and the images disband!
What bowl may catch these rose-cut stars unfolding
Casually brief electrons through my hand?

*Gwladys Downes*

## ✺ Vision

The woman looks out of the whale's bone
her eyes eroded
sinking
into the marrow
the source of vision.
The whale cutting
the water
sings like a huge machine.
all his bones
have eyes.

*Pat Lowther*


## ✺ Did

One thousand icebergs
in the sunlight around
the corner of New-
foundland, I saw

from the window
of a VC 10
& wisht William Blake
could have seen that.

I did

he said.

*George Bowering*

## 🌿 *The Dream*

I open the door from the bathroom
to the corridor. A small
blond child is standing there.
He looks at me.
"Who are you?" I ask. He says, "God."

*Tom Marshall*

## 🌿 *Benedictions*

For that he gave to a stone understanding to understand direction.
For that he made no slave for me.
For that he clothes the naked with the nudities of beasts.
For that he erects the contracted.
For that he smites me each dawn with a planet.

*A. M. Klein*

holy day is due holy day is
due holy day is due all th peopul
is one drum call do what yu
have to holy day is due holy
day is due holy day is due
all th peopul is one drum call
now do what yu have to holy
day is due holy day is due

*bill bissett*


## Arrival

The light goes out, the dark comes down,
Small cries, low murmurs of foxes.
A light descends on the trees, whitish like what
They themselves give off. Watching, I am moved
To prayer, to the crying out of titles
Of certain poems, the names of God,
My *own* name. It takes shape before me.
It is the night's name, my wife's name.
In motion, in one another's arms,
We arrive somewhere where none of this is so.

*Robert Sward*

## Sacred Enough You Are

Sacred enough you are.
Why should I praise
You, make you holier
Than is the case?
One does not wear
Phylacteries
On Sabbath days.

A. M. Klein

## my friends give me back feeling

maybe sumwhun will cum nd take us
away rescue us gathr us up together
all how ever many we are into covrd
wagons take us to where sumwhere
weve never herd of before deep
in the glowing woods she held my hand

bill bissett

## 🐾 Impasse

that I love you as softly
as a cat's fur quietly
as a feather & simply
as bread

      doesn't prevent
the claw from showing
the quill from pricking
nor the bread from burning

*Frederick Candelaria*

From the Sequence
*Living in the Moon*

## *The Song*

Body of flesh
that to me is
body of white bread
of the loaf's whiteness

she is
bread to me
she is bread to me

my fingers shaking
to touch such beauty
the white surface of

she is bread to me

*Tom Wayman*

## 🌿 *The Believable Body*

When
you give, it gives. Wherever you touch,
it touches back. And against your body
it feels like your body.

*C.H. Gervais*

O

her
blonde head
sunk between my
knees in grey bath water
her hair streaming long thick
strands reminds me
of sweetened
rhubarb

*C.H. Gervais*

## Measure

The lady little less
Than beautiful? Confess
That little less gives her the sort of
Beauty beauty falls short of.

*Robert Finch*


## Girl with Buck Teeth

I am a flower
Full of stones.
Passage is offered
Between my bones.

*Jay Macpherson*

### 𝕎 *Fingers*

The space I don't fill not placing
my fingers between yours.

  *Nelson Ball*

### 𝕎 *Flies*

tonight
in this room
two flies
on the ceiling
are making
love
quietly. Or

so it seems
down here

  *Phyllis Webb*

## ☙ *Invader*

A dark Gabriel he passed
    the burning bush
and entered her white house

Now there is no place
    nook nor corner
where she can be alone or call her own

    *Kay Smith*


## ☙ *Skeleton Wish*

You do not even crook your littlest finger
    yet my whole bone lies hooked there

    *Elizabeth Gourlay*

M. Antonius M.F. M.N.
remembered, as he went to bed,
the raiders rustling at the border,
the fields unfarmed, the towns unfed,
debts, and dejection, and disorder,

and, as he thumped and tussled there,
wondered how any man could prize
beyond the Roman world, a pair
of not so young Egyptian thighs.

*L. A. MacKay*

## *Judith Makes Comparisons*

Judith had heard a troubadour
singing beneath a castle-turret
Of truth, chivalry and honour,
Of virtue and of gallant merit,—
Judith had heard a troubadour
Lauding the parfait knightly spirit,
Singing beneath the ivied wall.
The cross-marked varlet Judith wrestled
Was not like these at all, at all . . .

*A. M. Klein*

## From the Chin P'ing Mei

Fifty men at arms with bows and lances
from the River Prefect. From the District Yamen
twenty more. Two hundred from General Chang.
The booms of drums, the clang of gongs—
She would have been frightened, my little one,
if she were alive and her palanquin,
passing through the South Gate at noonday,
had encountered the funeral procession
of a dead lady—she would have wept.

*Al Purdy*

## Communion

Naked, she wove herself into the ferns
her hair a glad welcome for butterflies.
I was her rich mould, her hidden nutriment
the musician of her strings.
I set her apart from the gold the green
                    the transparency.
My life in her shone out from her very eyes.

*Fernand Ouelette*
*Trans. F.R. Scott*

## 🌿 Complaint

You don't tell me much about the presents
    strange oriental men give you—
the twelve small dolls in a box,
    the tiny bowl of asparagus sprouts,
their thin green shoots pointing to the sky.

*John Newlove*


## 🌿 Low Calorie

I scatter more crumbs
for my black-capped chickadees
than you spread for me.

*Elizabeth Gourlay*

## The Refusal

I come to attention
between stillnesses.
I have heard it for a long time now—
the insistent rasp of tiny mouths
in the live rock.
Their sucking calls me.
The sand stretches out and I watch the gulls
cracking the backs of crabs.
You cracked me open and walked away
without breaking your perfect balance.
I watch my hands wait for each other,
refusing to know.

*Rosemary Sullivan*


## Refutation

Why did the famous poets lie to me?
Why did they tell me that the blood runs cold?
I, a simpleton, took them at their word
Who now by your grace am so wildly stirred
I shout like a madman from ecstasy,
My temples pounding though I am grey and old.

*Irving Layton*

## Love-Song II of Jenny Lear

Were I a Shakespearian daughter,
Safe restored through fire and water,
You the party in the crown
—Someone get the curtain down.

*Jay Macpherson*




## Impresa

Iron on iron: and so we sharpen
each other's countenance;

Skin to skin: so we kindle
each day's heart.

*Alexander Hutchison*

## Yours

It lay unfolded upward on my knee
Armed five wise ways like Shiva for the dance.
Cross-lined for life, for love, for coming fate,
Warm, as I matched it with my own right hand.

F.R. Scott


## Winter at Roblin Lake

Seeing the sky darken & the fields
turn brown & the lake lead-grey
as some enormous scrap of sheet metal
& wind grabs the world around the equator
I am most thankful then for knowing about
        the little gold hairs on your belly

Al Purdy

After so much change, so little change;
After so much lost love, so lost a lover.
Now while the quiet seconds slip away
Into a hastening absence, it is strange,
Stranger than all believing, to discover
Nothing to say, and nothing to unsay.

*L. A. MacKay*

 *Us Together*

I do not like anything the way I
like you in your underwear I like you
and in your party clothes o my in your
party clothes and with nothing on at all
you do not need to wear a thing at all
for me to like you and you may talk or
not talk I like you either way nothing
makes me feel so nearly at home on Earth
as just to be with you and say nothing.

*George Johnston*

The lights go out as you enter
you are the light inside me

The light blinds me
now I can see in my blindness

I can see the secret face I saw
at my birth before time fitted me
with special distorting lenses

> *Kay Smith*

 From *Translations from the Japanese*

O fireflies gather
long enough
to show his face
who speaks to me

> *W. W. E. Ross*

## Song

I almost went to bed
without remembering
the four white violets
I put in the buttonhole
of your green sweater

and how I kissed you then
and you kissed me
shy as though I'd
never been your lover

*Leonard Cohen*


## For Anne

With Annie gone,
whose eyes to compare
with the morning sun?

Not that I did compare,
But I do compare
Now that she's gone.

*Leonard Cohen*

## Nightgown, Wife's Gown

Where do people go when they go to sleep?
I envy them. I want to go there too.
I am outside of them, married to them.
Nightgown, wife's gown, women that you look at,
Beside them—I knock on their shoulder blades
Ask to be let in. It is forbidden.
But you're my wife, I say. There is no reply.
Arms around her, I caress her wings.

*Robert Sward*

## The Infernal Compliment

When two bodies come
                    together a
certain sound arises


If nature says this is
                    not to be
they must never touch


The space between
                    them must always
remain harmonious

*Doug Beardsley*

## 🐟 *Element*

My love
you are but a common metallic element

I need you
where resistance to heat is essential

I seize
your contumacious ductile body

I mix you
with caustic salts & dissociate acids

I use you
in the manufacture of tart alloys

I call you
Tantalum

*Doug Beardsley*

## 𝕏 *hubble's constant*

at night
I put my hand
on your red

shift
where it curves
around your breast

the light
years are still

there

*D. M. Price*

## 🌾 *That Time I Saw Einstein*

How lively the old man's eyes!
a cosmonaut getting younger
with every cast of mind around his universe.

*R. G. Everson*

## 🌾 *The Taste of Space*

McLuhan put his telescope to his ear;
What a lovely smell, he said, we have here.

*A. J. M. Smith*

🪶 *washed ashore on a beach in british columbia*
*and found when i checked to see*
*if the beer was still cold*

dear st andreas

it's your fault
there was an earthquake

sincerely
l.a.

D.M. Price


🪶 *Political Digression*

I saw two go by
like dragon-flies
      joined

a kind of
  intercourse
from tail
to thorax—

the dry whisk
of eight beating
wings

*Alexander Hutchison*

## General Election 1935

There is nothing like hard times
For teaching a people to think.
By a decisive vote
After discussing all the issues
They have turned out the Conservatives
And put back the Liberals.

> F. R. Scott

## East and West

In this country I speak freely, without fear;
But no one in this lethargy will ever hear.

Back *there*, all listen to what I have to say;
Especially the secret police, who lead me away.

> George Faludy
> Trans. John Robert Colombo

## Charity

A code of laws
Lies written
On this beggar's hand.

My small coin
Lengthens
The harsh sentence.

*F.R. Scott*

## Lines for a Cynic

A lofty stare. A fat behind.
These guard the opinions of mankind.

'I am hungry.' 'I have dined.'
These summarize the human mind.

*Gael Turnbull*

## 🎋 Of Beauty

Seeing that planets move by dynamos,
And even the sun's a burnished well-oiled spring,
What glory is there, say, in being a rose
And why should skylarks still desire to sing,
Singing, and no men hear, men standing close
Over some sleek, mechanic and vociferous thing?

For these there is one beauty; put it on a table:
A loaf of bread, some salt, a vegetable.

    *A. M. Klein*


## 🎋 In Rattlesnake Country

I am not afraid
of that rattler.

What's its poor venom
compared to that of a human?

    *Irving Layton*

## Truce

My enemy in a purple hat
looks suddenly like a plum
and I am dumb with wonder
at the thought
of feuding with a fruit

*P.K. Page*


## Time to Kill

At the corner of First and Last a woman I know stops me Have you
got a minute she asks me I give
her what I have she uses
it I get it
back 2 hours late—
r second
hand.

*Helene Rosenthal*

## 🐦 De-Composition

A golden tooth within the buck-
mouthed prairie town the yellow
stiff hotel is stuck and stuck
within it like a deadened
nerve a thin gray wai-
tress drones the bill-of-fare
to one pained salesman for enamelware

   *Earle Birney*


## 🐦 Degeneration

The first to go are the niceties,
The little minor conformities
That suddenly seem absurdities.

Soon kindling animosities
Surmount the old civilities
And start the first brutalities.

Then come the bold extremities,
The justified enormities,
The unrestrained ferocities.

   *F.R. Scott*

## ❧ Vaughan's World

I saw eternity the other day
Most like a ring of drab unending grey.
"Look! there's eternity!" said my mother-in-law.
"Yes, Mother," said my wife. "We know. We saw."

*Francis Sparshott*


## ❧ 1900

On the twenty-fifth of August God said
Nietzsche is dead.

*Francis Sparshott*


## ❧ Mausoleum Hunting: Ravenna

Theodoric, the Emperor,
One night, the lid off,
was dispersed by
A little wind.

*Ralph Gustafson*

## 🌿 Dust

Dust floats
in the sunlit air

comes to rest
in layers

a fine
fur

lining
our rooms.

*Nelson Ball*

## 🌿 Carthorses
## on the Kuse Rd.

the horses
on the road
running
to dust

*Allan Safarik*

## 𓆝 Kakuyu Print

The man walks past the
Flower. Frogs slap their sides, the
Hare rolls with laughter.

*Ralph Gustafson*

## 𓆝 Breakfast II

Nijinsky's spirit dances over
on eight sprightly legs
towards the cosmonaut
glued on a parachute
and I become
a breakfast for a dancer.

*Joe Rosenblatt*

## A Long Line Of Baby Caterpillars

A long line of baby caterpillars
follow their leader from the house corner
heading dead on for the Japanese Plum Tree.

Take away my wisdom and my categories.

*Phyllis Webb*

## Style

This last July a crazy caterpillar
Displayed a miniature raccoon-coat; and
This late October I discovered him
Frigidly lying on a bed of state,
Attired in ermine.

*A. M. Klein*

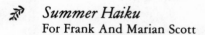

### July Creatures

After the dim blue rain
swarms of innocent flying things
(green things, curly-bodied things,
things shaped like an arrowhead)
tiny with outsize wings

go wherever the wind wobbles
among pinwheeling swallows
and meet uncomprehended harm
in blonde thickets on my forearm.

*Milton Acorn*


### Summer Haiku
For Frank And Marian Scott

Silence

and a deeper silence

when the crickets

hesitate

*Leonard Cohen*

listen

listen

listen

silent

*Stephen Scobie*

# Acknowledgements

Grateful acknowledgement is made to the following authors, publishers, copyright holders and literary executors for kind permission to reproduce the poems in this book:

Milton Acorn for "More Intricate" and "July Creatures" from *I've Tasted My Blood*, Steel Rail Press. Courtesy of the author.

Margaret Atwood for 'you fit into me' from *Power Politics*, House of Anansi, copyright © Margaret Atwood 1971. Reprinted by permission of the author and the publisher.

Nelson Ball for "Fingers" from *Made in Canada*, Oberon Press, 1970; "Dust" and "February" from *Points of Attention*, 1971. All reprinted by permission of the author.

Maxwell Bates for "Life Work" from *Far-Away Flags*, The Seymour Press Limited, copyright © Maxwell Bates 1964. Reprinted by permission of the author.

Doug Beardsley for "Voices," "Fall," "Infernal Compliment" and "Element." Reprinted by permission of the author.

Earle Birney for "De-Compositon" and "Ellesmereland" from *The Collected Poems*, 2 volumes, 1975, copyright © by Earle Birney. Reprinted by permission of the author and The Canadian Publishers, McClelland and Stewart Limited, Toronto.

bill bissett for 'holy day is due' from *Nobody Owns the Earth*, House of Anansi, copyright © 1971 by bill bissett, and for "my friends give me back feeling" from *lost angel mining company*. Reprinted by permission of the author.

George Bowering for "Did" from *Cross Country*. "Play Among the Stars" and "The Frost" from *Touch* by George Bowering reprinted by permission of The Canadian Publishers, McClelland and Stewart Limited, Toronto. "First Night of Fall, Grosvenor Ave." from *How Do I Love Thee* edited by John Robert Colombo, Hurtig Publishers, 1970. Reprinted by permission of the author.

Elizabeth Brewster for "Munchausen in Alberta," "Fog" and "Alchemist" from *Sunrise North* by Elizabeth Brewster, copyright © 1972 by Clarke, Irwin & Company Limited. Used by permission.

Fred Candelaria for "Impasse" from *Malahat Review*. Courtesy of the author.

Leonard Cohen for "Summer Haiku", "Song" and "For Anne" from *Spice-Box of Earth*, 1961. Reprinted by permission of The Canadian Publishers, McClelland and Stewart Limited, Toronto, and the author.

Don Coles for permission to reprint "Running Child".

John Robert Colombo for permission to reprint "The Sibyl at Cumae" (found in the screenplay to Fellini's *Satyricon*, 1969); the translations of "A Cat" by Jacques Godbout and "East and West" by George Faludy.

Jeni Couzyn for permission to reprint "Love" from *Flying* and "Grace for Snow" from *Christmas in Africa*, J.J. Douglas, copyright © 1975 Jeni Couzyn.

Gwladys Downes for "A Drink in the Luxembourg" from *Out of the Violent Dark*, Sono Nis Press, copyright © 1978 Gwladys Downes.

Mike Doyle for permission to use "Corridor Smiles", "Of Skies" and "Moon Phases".

Louis Dudek for permission to reprint "Spaces" from *The Transparent Sea*, Contact Press, copyright © 1956 Louis Dudek, "Poetry for Intellectuals" from *Laughing Stalks*, copyright © 1958 Louis Dudek, and "Tree in a Street" from *East of the City*, Ryerson Press.

R. G. Everson for permission to reprint "View of a Madhouse", "Illusion from my Speedy Car", "Farewell" and "That Time I Saw Einstein".

George Faludy for "East and West", translated by John Robert Colombo.

Robert Finch for "Measure" from *The Strength of the Hills*, copyright © 1948 by The Canadian Publishers, McClelland and Stewart Limited, Toronto. Reprinted by permission of the publisher. "Aria Senza da Capo" reprinted by permission of the author from *Acis in Oxford and Other Poems* by Robert Finch, University of Toronto Press, 1961.

R.A.D. Ford for permission to reprint "Witness to my Body" from *Tamarack Review*.

Gail Fox for permission to reprint "Sunstroke. 1954" from *The Royal Collector of Dreams* by Gail Fox, Fiddlehead Poetry Books, copyright © by Gail Fox 1970.

C.H. Gervais for permission to reprint "The Believable Body", "O" and "Falling Star".

Roland Giguere for "Greener than Nature" from *Poems of French Canada*, translated by F.R. Scott, Blackfish Press, copyright © by F.R. Scott. Reprinted by permission of the author and translator.

John Glassco for permission to reprint lines 91 and 92 of his translation of *Epitre a Monsieur Labadie* by Joseph Quesnel.

Jacques Godbout for permission to publish in a slightly revised version "A Cat" from *How Do I Love Thee*, edited by John Robert Colombo, Hurtig Publishers, 1970.

Phyllis Gotlieb for permission to reprint 'Tiretracks' from *The Works* by Phyllis Gotlieb, Calliope Press.

Elizabeth Gourlay for permission to reprint "Low Calorie" from *Motions, Dreams & Aberrations*, Morris Printing Company, copyright © 1969 by Elizabeth Gourlay.

Eldon Grier for permission to reprint 'I am almost asleep' from *A Friction of Lights*, Contact Press, 1963.

Ralph Gustafson for "Mausoleum Hunting: Ravenna" from *Selected Poems*, copyright © 1972 by Ralph Gustafson; and "Kakuyu Print" from *Fire on Stone*, copyright © 1974 by Ralph Gustafson. Reprinted by permission of The Canadian Publishers, McClelland and Stewart Limited, Toronto, and the author.

Anne Hebert for "Snow" from *St-Denis Garneau and Anne Hebert* Translations by F.R. Scott, Klanak Press, copyright © 1962 F.R. Scott.

Robert Hogg for permission to reprint "Song" from *The Connexions* by Robert Hogg, 1966.

Alexander Hutchison for "Political Digression" and "Impresa" from *Deep-Tap Tree*, University of Massachusetts Press, 1978, copyright © by Alexander Hutchison. Reprinted by permission of the publisher and author.

Waclaw Iwaniuk for permission to reprint "They Say I do not Suffer", translated by Jagna Boraks, from *Tamarack Review*.

George Johnston for "O Earth, Turn", "Us Together", "Deep", "Catpath", "The Street in Fall" and "Ongoing" from *Happy Enough* by George Johnston, copyright © Oxford University Press (Canadian Branch), 1972; and "Frost" from *The Wind has Wings*, compiled by Mary Alice Downey and Barbara Robertson, Oxford University Press (Canadian branch). Reprinted by permission of author and publisher.

D.G. Jones for permission to reprint "The Wind Disturbs" from *The Sun is Axeman*, University of Toronto Press (permission also granted by publisher), 'No temple or palace' from *Frost on the Sun*, Contact Press, copyright © 1957 by D.G. Jones.

Penny Kemp for permission to reprint "Stabilities" from *Bearing Down*, Coach House Press, 1977.

Leo Kennedy for permission to reprint "Mad Boy's Song" from *The Shrouding*.

A.M. Klein, "Sacred Enough You Are", "Judith Makes Comparisons", "Benedictions", "Of Beauty", "Style", "Of Nothing at All: Orders", "Ni la Mort ni le Soleil" and "Aesthetic Curiosity" from *The Collected Poems of A.M. Klein* compiled by Miriam Waddington. Copyright © McGraw-Hill Ryerson Limited, 1974. Reprinted by permission of publisher and Sandor and Colman Klein.

Raymond Knister, "Lake Harvest" from *The Collected Poems of Raymond Knister*. Reprinted by permission of McGraw-Hill Ryerson Limited.

Patrick Lane for permission to reprint "White Mountain" from *Poems New & Selected* by Patrick Lane, Oxford University Press. Copyright © 1978 by Patrick Lane.

Irving Layton for "Epigram for A.M. Klein" from *The Unwavering Eye* by Irving Layton, "Refutation" from *Lovers and Lesser Men* by Irving Layton, "In Rattlesnake Country", "Prussian Blue" and "Divine Image" from *The Collected Poems of Irving Layton*, copyright © 1971 by Irving Layton. Reprinted by permission of The Canadian Publishers, McClelland and Stewart Limited, Toronto, and the author.

Dorothy Livesay for permission to reprint "The Cabbage"; and "Going to Sleep" from *Collected Poems* by Dorothy Livesay, McGraw-Hill Ryerson Limited. Copyright © 1972 by Dorothy Livesay. Reprinted by permission.

Malcolm Lowry, "Strange Type", "Epitaph", "Nocturne in Burrard Inlet", "The Search" and "Trinity". Copyright © 1962 by Margerie Lowry. Reprinted by permission of Margerie Lowry and City Lights Books, San Francisco.

Pat Lowther, "Vision" from *Milkstone* by Pat Lowther. Copyright © by Borealis Press Limited. Reprinted by permission of publisher, and the estate of Patricia Lowther.

Gwendolyn MacEwen for 'with legs and arms I make alphabets' from the sequence "Poems in Braille" from *Magic Animals*, by Gwendolyn MacEwen. Reprinted by permission of The Macmillan Company of Canada.

L.A. MacKay for permission to reprint "M. Antonius" and 'After so much change'. Part of "Outmoded Wisdom—Cleobulus" from *The Blasted Pine* by L.A. MacKay, edited by F.R. Scott and A.J.M. Smith, reprinted by permission of The Macmillan Company of Canada Limited.

Jay Macpherson for permission to reprint "The Well" and "Poets & Muses" from *Welcoming Disaster* by Jay Macpherson, Saanes Publications. Copyright © 1974 by Jay Macpherson. "The Plowman in Darkness", "The Third Eye", "Go Take the World", "Egg" and "Reader" from *The Boatman* by Jay Macpherson, Oxford University Press, 1957; "Girl with Buck Teeth" and "Love Song II of Jenny Lear" from *The Boatman and Other Poems* by Jay Macpherson, Oxford University Press, copyright © 1968 by Jay Macphrson, reprinted by permission of author and publisher.

Eli Mandel for permission to reprint "Streetlights" from *An Idiot Joy* by Eli Mandel, copyright © 1967 by Eli Mandel, Hurtig Publishers.

John Marshall for permission to reprint "Seymour Inlet Float Camp: Domestic Scene" from *Skookum Wawa*, edited by Gary Geddes, Oxford University Press, 1975; also in *Saltspring*, *Oolichan Books, 1979*.

Tom Marshall for "The Dream" which has been reprinted from *The Earth-Book* by kind permission of Oberon Press.

David McFadden for "Keys". Courtesy of the author.

Floris Clark McLaren, "Field in the Wind" from *Frozen Fire* by Floris Clark McLaren, The Macmillan Company of Canada Limited, 1937. Courtesy of Bruce McLaren.

Rona Murray for 'After all'. Courtesy of the author.

Emile Nelligan, "The Muse's Cradle", translated by P.F. Widdows, from *Selected Poems of Emile Nelligan*, Ryerson Press. Courtesy of P.F. Widdows.

John Newlove for "Complaint". Courtesy of the author.

bpNichol for "Blues" from *Concrete Poetry: A World View* edited by Mary Ellen Solt, Indiana University Press, 1968. Courtesy of the author.

Alden Nowlan for "Unfinished Poem" from *I'm a Stranger Here Myself* by Alden Nowlan, copyright © 1974 by Clarke, Irwin & Company Limited. Used by Permission. "Aunt Jane" and "Biography" reprinted courtesy of the author.

Howard O'Hagan for "For Margaret". Courtesy of the author.

Michael Ondaatje for "Fabulous Shadow" from *Rat Jelly* by Michael Ondaatje, Coach House Press, copyright © 1973 by Michael Ondaatje.

Fernand Ouelette for "Communion", translated by F.R. Scott, from *The Poetry of French Canada* edited by John Glassco, Oxford University Press, 1970. Courtesy of the author and translator.

Richard Outram for permission to reprint "Story" from *Turns and Other Poems* by Richard Outram, Anson Cartwright Editions, copyright © 1975 by Richard Outram.

P.K. Page for "Stefan" from *Vancouver Island Poems* edited by Robert Sward, Soft Press, 1973; "On Brushing my Hair in the Static-Filled Air" from *Malahat Review*, Jan. 1978; "Truce" from *Poems Selected and New* by P.K. Page, House of Anansi Press, copyright © 1974 by P.K. Page.

D.M. Price for "hubble's constant", "moon: tracks" and "washed ashore on a beach in british columbia and found when i checked to see if the beer was still cold". Courtesy of the author.

Al Purdy for "Mice in the House" from *Cariboo Horses* by Al Purdy, "Winter at Roblin Lake" and "From the Chin P'ing Mei" from *Selected Poems* by Al Purdy, copyright © 1972 by Al Purdy, reprinted by permission of The Canadian Publishers, McClelland and Stewart Limited, Toronto, and the author.

Joseph Quesnel, 'Say, Artist' from *Epitre a Monsieur Labadie* by Joseph Quesnel, translated by John Glassco. Courtesy of the translator.

James Reaney for permission to reprint "The Tree" from *Poetry*, December 1969, also in *Selected Shorter Poems*, Press Porcepic, copyright © by James Reaney. "Suns and Planets" and "The Hat" from *Poems* by James Reaney, new press, 1972, copyright © by James Reaney. Reprinted by permission of the author and publisher.

Goodridge Roberts for 'Cezanne at last' from *Preview*, May 1942. Courtesy of Mrs. G. Roberts.

Joe Rosenblatt for "Breakfast 11" from *The LSD Leacock* by Joe Rosenblatt and also in *Topsoil*, Press Porcepic, copyright © 1976 by Joe Rosenblatt. Courtesy of the author and publisher.

Helene Rosenthal for "Time to Kill" from *Listen to the Old Mother* by Helene Rosenthal, reprinted by permission of the Canadian Publishers, McClelland and Stewart Limited, Toronto.

W.W.E. Ross, "Let Us Rebuild", 'The fireflies' and 'O fireflies gather' from "Translations from the Japanese" published in *Shapes and Sounds* by W.W.E. Ross, selected by Raymond Souster and John Robert Colombo, Longmans (Canada) Limited, copyright © 1968 by Mary Lowry Ross.

Allan Safarik for "Carthorses on the Kuse Rd." Courtesy of the author.

Stephen Scobie for 'listen/silent' from *In the Silence of the Year*, Delta. Courtesy of the author.

F.R. Scott for permission to reprint "Is", "Yes and No", "Degeneration" and "Eclipse" from *Signature* by F.R. Scott, Klanak Press, copyright © 1964 by F.R. Scott; "Charity" from *Events and Signals*, Ryerson Press, 1954; "General Election 1935" from *The Eye of the Needle* by F.R. Scott, Contact Press, 1957; and "Epitaph". "Yours", "Winter Sparrows", "Greener than Nature" by Roland Giguere, tr. by F.R. Scott, and "Communion" by Fernand Ouelette, tr. by F.R. Scott, from *The Dance is One*, copyright © 1973 by F.R. Scott, reprinted by permission of F.R. Scott, The Canadian Publishers, McClelland and Stewart Limited, Toronto, and the authors. "Snow" by Anne Hebert from *St-Denis Garneau and Anne Hebert* Translations by F.R. Scott, Klanak Press, copyright © 1962 F.R. Scott. Courtesy of the author and translator.

Joseph Sherman for "First and Last". Courtesy of the author.

Robin Skelton for permission to reprint 'I too am a student' from *A Difficult Mountain*, Kayak Books, 1972.

A.J.M. Smith for permission to publish for the first time 'From little sorrows' and to reprint "To Jay Macpherson On Her Book of Poems" from *Poems New & Collected* by A.J.M. Smith, Oxford University Press, 1967, and also in *The Classic Shade*, The Canadian Publishers, McClelland and Stewart, Toronto, copyright © 1978 by A.J.M. Smith; "Two Sides of a Drum", "The Taste of Space" from *Poems New & Collected;* and "Beside One Dead" from *News of the Phoenix and Other Poems*, Ryerson Press, 1943.

Kay Smith for permission to reprint "At the Bottom of the Dark", 'The lights go out as you enter', "Like a Garment" and "Invader" from *At the Bottom of the Dark*, Fiddlehead, 1971, copyright © by Kay Smith.

Francis Sparshott for permission to use "The Cloud", "Vaughan's World" and "1900".

Rosemary Sullivan for permission to use "The Reborn" and "The Refusal".

Robert Sward for permission to reprint "Oppression", "Hannah", "Arrival" and "Nightgown, Wife's Gown" from *Thousand-Year-Old Fiancee*, Cornell University Press, 1965, copyright © 1979 by Robert Sward.

Colleen Thibaudeau for "Bell" and "The Top" from *Lozenges*, by Colleen Thibaudeau, Alphabet Press, 1965.

Gael Turnbull for permission to reprint "A Dying Man", "Lines for a Bookmark" and "Lines for a Cynic" from *Trio*, Contact Press, 1945, copyright © Gael Turnbull.

Jean Vanier for 'How many times'. Courtesy of Griffin House Press.

Miriam Waddington for "Anxious" from *Driving Home* by Miriam Waddington, copyright © 1972 by Oxford University Press, and "We Are Not One" from *The Price of Gold* by Miriam Waddington, Oxford University Press, copyright © 1976 Miriam Waddington. Courtesy of the author and publisher.

Fred Wah for permission to reprint "Song" from *Among*, Coach House Press.

Tom Wayman for "The Song" from the sequence "Living in the Moon" published in *For and Against the Moon*. Reprinted by permission of the author and The Macmillan Company of Canada Limited.

Phyllis Webb for permission to reprint 'star fish' and "Flies" from *Naked Poems*, Periwinkle Press, copyright © 1965 Phyllis Webb; 'my white skin', "Sitting" and "A Long Line of Baby Caterpillars" from *The Sea is Also a Garden*, 1962.

Anne Wilkinson, 'Poets are fishermen' and 'Poets are cool as the divers' from *Three Poems About Poets*, courtesy of Alan Wilkinson. "La Belle Dame sans dormi", "Old Adam" and "If you should die" from *The Collected Poems of Anne Wilkinson* by Anne Wilkinson, edited by A.J.M. Smith, reprinted by permission of The Macmillan Company of Canada Limited.

George Woodcock for permission to publish "On a Cat's Portrait" and to reprint "A Farmer's Epitaph" and "Binaries: 'Soul clap your hands'" from *Notes on Visitations: Poems 1936-1975*, copyright © 1975 by George Woodcock.

X for "XXX" from *The McGill Fortnightly Review, 1926*.

J. Michael Yates for permission to reprint 'The wolves say to the dogs' from *The Great Bear Lake Meditations* by J. Michael Yates.

Ian Young for "A Dream" Courtesy of the author.

Robert Zend for "Morning" and "Requiescat". From *Zero to One*. Sono Nis Press, 1973. Reprinted by permission of the publisher, author.

Care has been taken to trace ownership of copyright material used in this book. Should there be any errors or omissions the publishers would be grateful for information that will make rectification possible in subsequent editions.

# Author-Title Index

Acorn, Milton, 18, 120
*Aesthetic Curiosity*, 60
*After all*, 42
*After so much change*, 102
*Alchemist*, 44
*Anxious*, 45
*Aria Senza da Capo*, 36
*Aristocratic Trio, An*, 74
*Arrival*, 88
*At the Bottom of the Dark*, 53
Atwood, Margaret, 29
*Aunt Jane*, 35

Ball, Nelson, 68, 94, 117
Bates, Maxwell, 70
Beardsley, Doug, 46, 61, 106, 107
*Believable Body, The*, 92
*Bell*, 77
*Belle Dame sans dormi, La*, 25
*Benedictions*, 87
*Beside One Dead*, 40
*Biography*, 18
Birney, Earle, 52, 115
bissett, bill, 88, 89
*Blues*, 29
Boraks, Jagna, 32
Bowering, George, 10, 59, 61, 86
*Breakfast II*, 118
Brewster, Elizabeth, 21, 44, 62

*Cabbage, The*, 51
*Canada in Winter*, 65
Candelaria, Fred, 90
*Carthorses on the Kuse Rd.*, 117
*Cat, A*, 69
*Catpath*, 68
Cezanne at last, 70
*Charity*, 112
*Cloud, The*, 44
Cohen, Leonard, 104, 120
Coles, Don, 83
Colombo, John Robert, 36, 69, 111
*Communion*, 97
*Complaint*, 98
*Corridor Smiles*, 46
Couzyn, Jeni, 25, 75

*De-Composition*, 115

*Deep*, 66
*Degeneration*, 115
*Did*, 86
*Divine Image*, 28
Downes, Gwladys, 85
Doyle, Mike, 10, 23, 46
*Dream, A*, 26
*Dream, The*, 87
*Drink in the Luxembourg, A*, 85
Dudek, Louis, 11, 16, 56
*Dust*, 117
*Dying Man, A*, 37

*East and West*, 111
*Eclipse*, 22
*Egg*, 76
*Element*, 107
*Ellesmereland*, 52
*Epigram for A.M. Klein*, 73
*Epitaph*
   by Malcolm Lowry, 39
   by F.R. Scott, 71
Everson, R.G., 31, 51, 83, 109

*Fabulous Shadow*, 28
*Fall*, 61
*Falling Star*, 11
Faludy, George, 111
*Farewell*, 83
*Farmer's Epitaph, A*, 39
*February*, 68
*Field in the Wind*, 52
Finch, Robert, 36, 93
*Fingers*, 94
*fireflies, The*, 26
*First and Last*, 43
*First Night of Fall, Grosvenor Ave.*, 59
*Flies*, 94
*Fog*, 21
*For Anne*, 104
Ford, R.A.D., 49
*For Margaret*, 80
Fox, Gail, 20
France, Judson, 74
*From little sorrows*, 33
*From the Chin P'ing Mei*, 97
*Frost*, 65
*Frost, The*, 61

General Election 1935, 111
Gervais, C.H., 11, 92
Giguere, Roland, 45
Girl with Buck Teeth, 93
Glassco, John, 72
Godbout, Jacques, 69
Going to Sleep, 41
'Go Take the World', 78
Gotlieb, Phyllis, 67
Gore, Deborah, 14, 41
Gourlay, Elizabeth, 35, 95, 98
Grace for Snow, 25
Greener Than Nature, 45
Grier, Eldon, 15
Gustafson, Ralph, 116, 118

Hanging, 35
Hannah, 84
Hat, The, 55
Hébert, Anne, 64
Hoffman, Jill, 65
Hogg, Robert, 54
holy day is due, 88
How many times, 47
hubble's constant, 108
Hutchison, Alexander, 100, 110

I am almost asleep, 15
If you should die, 37
Illusion from my Speedy Car, 51
Impasse, 90
Impresa, 100
Infernal Compliment, The, 106
In Rattlesnake Country, 113
Invader, 95
Is, 79
I too am a student, 43
Iwaniuk, Waclaw, 32

Johnston, George, 38, 50, 60, 65, 66, 68, 102
Jones, D.G., 53, 54
Judith Makes Comparisons, 96
July Creatures, 120

Kakuyu Print, 118
Kemp, Penny, 31
Kennedy, Leo, 32
Keys, 13
Klein, A.M., 22, 60, 73, 79, 87, 89, 96, 113, 119
Knister, Raymond, 63

Lake Harvest, 63
Lane, Patrick, 66
Layton, Irving, 28, 73, 74, 99, 113
Let Us Rebuild, 71
Life Work, 70
lights go out as you enter, The, 103
Like a Garment, 27
Lines for a Bookmark, 76
Lines for a Cynic, 112
listen, 121
Livesay, Dorothy, 41, 51
Long Line of Baby Caterpillars, A, 119
Love, 75
Love-Song II of Jenny Lear, 100
Low Calorie, 98
Lowry, Malcolm, 33, 34, 39, 58
Lowther, Pat, 86

MacEwen, Gwendolyn, 50
MacKay, L.A., 72, 96, 102
Macpherson, Jay, 17, 24, 76, 78, 81, 85, 9
100
Mad Boy's Song, 32
Mandel, Eli, 58
M. Antonius M.F. M.N., 96
Marshall, John, 30
Marshall, Tom, 87
Mausoleum Hunting: Ravenna, 116
McFadden, David, 13
McLaren, Floris Clark, 52
Measure, 93
Mice in the House, 15
Moon Phases, 23
moon: tracks, 23
More Intricate, 18
Morning, 47
Munchausen in Alberta, 62
Murray, Rona, 42
Muses' Cradle, The, 17
my friends give me back feeling, 89
My white skin, 27

Nelligan, Emile, 17
Newman, Jerry, 16, 38
Newlove, John, 98
Nichol, bp, 29
Nightgown, Wife's Gown, 105
Ni la Mort ni le Soleil, 22
1900, 116
Nocturne in Burrard Inlet, 58
No temple or palace, 54
Nowlan, Alden, 18, 35, 42

O, 92
O Earth, Turn!, 50
Of Beauty, 113
Of Faith, Hope, and Charity, 73
O fireflies gather, 103
Of Nothing at All: Orders, 79
Of Skies, 10
O'Hagan, Howard, 80
Old Adam, 82
On a Cat's Portrait, 69
On Brushing my Hair in the Static-Filled Air, 49
Ondaatje, Michael, 28
Ongoing, 38
Oppression, 30
Ouelette, Fernand, 97
Outram, Richard, 81

Page, P.K., 49, 84, 114
Pattern, 59
Play Among the Stars, 10
Plowman in Darkness, The, 24
Poetry, 16
Poetry for Intellectuals, 16
Poets & Muses, 17
Poets are cool as the divers who wander, 19
Poets are fishermen crying, 14
Political Digression, 110
Price, D.M., 23, 108, 110
Prussian Blue, 74
Purdy, Al, 15, 97, 101

Quesnel, Joseph, 72

Razor Blade, 41
Reaney, James, 12, 13, 55
Reborn, The, 82
Refusal, The, 99
Refutation, 99
Requiescat, 40
Roberts, Goodridge, 70
Rosenblatt, Joe, 118
Rosenthal, Helene, 114
Ross, W.W.E., 26, 71, 103
Running Child, 83

Sacred Enough You Are, 89
Safarik, Allan, 117
Say, Artist, what's the hardest sentence known?, 72
Schenk, Christian, 19
Scobie, Stephen, 121

Scott, F.R., 22, 45, 64, 67, 71, 75, 79, 97, 101, 111, 112, 115
Search, The, 34
Seymour Inlet Float Camp: Domestic Scene, 30
Sherman, Joseph, 43
Sibyl at Cumae, The, 36
Sickness unto Death, The, 38
Sitting, 21
Skeleton Wish, 95
Skelton, Robin, 43
Smith, A.J.M., 33, 40, 78, 80, 109
Smith, Kay, 27, 53, 95, 103
Snow, 64
Song
    by Leonard Cohen, 104
    by Robert Hogg, 54
    by Fred Wah, 56
Song, The, 91
Soul, clap your hands, 24
Spaces, 11
Sparshott, Francis, 44, 116
Stabilities, 31
star fish, 9
Stefan, 84
Story, 81
Strange Type, 34
Street in Fall, The, 60
Streetlights, 58
Style, 119
Sullivan, Rosemary, 82, 99
Summer Haiku, 120
Suns and Planets, 13
sunshine is the glee, The, 19
Sunstroke. 1954, 20
Sward, Robert, 30, 84, 88, 105

Taste of Space, The, 109
That Time I Saw Einstein, 109
They Say I do not Suffer, 32
Thibaudeau, Colleen, 77
Third Eye, The, 85
This is Not, 14
Time to Kill, 114
Tiretracks, 67
To bring mine enemy down in black despair, 72
To Jay Macpherson On Her Book of Poems, 78
Top, The, 77
Tree in a Street, 56
Tree, The, 12
Trinity, 33

*Truce,* 114
Turnbull, Gael, 37, 76, 112
*Two Sides of a Drum, The,* 80

Ulrich, W.D., 59
*Unfinished Poem,* 42
*Us Together,* 102

Vanier, Jean, 47
*Vaughan's World,* 116
*View of a Madhouse,* 31
*Vision,* 86
*Voices,* 46

Waddington, Miriam, 45, 48
Wah, Fred, 56
*washed ahsore on a beach in british columbia,* 110
Wayman, Tom, 91
*We are not One,* 48
Webb, Phyllis, 9, 21, 27, 94, 119
*Well, The,* 81

*White Mountain,* 66
Widdows, P.F., 17
Wilkinson, Anne, 14, 19, 25, 37, 82
*Wind Disturbs, The,* 53
*Winter at Roblin Lake,* 101
*Winter Sparrows,* 67
with legs and arms I make alphabets, 50
*Witness to my Body,* 49
wolves say to the dogs, The, 48
Woodcock, George, 24, 39, 69

X, 57
*XXX,* 57

Yates, J. Michael, 48
*Yes and No,* 75
you fit into me, 29
Young, Ian, 26
*Yours,* 101

Zend, Robert, 40, 47